12 Step Reader

Thoughts, Prayers and Meditations

Compiled by Tom M.

Photographs by Lloyd Sagendorph

12 Step Reader

First Edition
August 23, 2013
Fifth printing and revisions February 2017

Published by CreateSpace.com
Available on Amazon.com

Dedicated to all those who have been part of my recovery, especially my wife, and to all those who are still sick and suffering

12 Step Reader

Introduction

I have come by these items as friends have shared their
thoughts with me, some from books, pamphlets, hand-
outs, and sheets of paper containing prayers and pearls
of wisdom. I tucked them into my daily reader.

Over time I have added my own thoughts, written my
reactions, or edited what I was given to suit my
situations and experiences. I have added quotes from
books I have read as well as written what I gleaned from
them or lecturers I have heard, or people I have met. I
have jotted in the margins, and filled the blank side of
the pages, written on the inside covers or anywhere
there was space, as thoughts occurred to me.

The result is a dog-eared collection of smudged papers,
and a bulging daily reader whose binding is giving way.
This led me to transcribing it all into a volume. Once
completed, it seemed to make sense to share it. I hope
you can find some of the peace and understanding I
have found in these pages.

Table of Contents

Chapter 1
Daily Prayers

Chapter 2
Meditations

Chapter 5
A Way of Life

Chapter 1

Daily Prayers

12 Step Reader

Thank you for this morning

I welcome this new day. It is your gift to me.

I thank you for the gift of being alive this morning, with its fresh air, its pending sunshine, its wonderful aromas and sounds. It's the birth of another day.

I thank you for giving me a day in which I can choose to be tolerant and patient, calm and accepting.

Thank you for the sleep which has refreshed me, and for the chance to begin all over again. If my sleep was fitful, help me to deal with my day in a positive way, and accept it as just the way it is. Allow me to be less anxious so tonight I may rest.

This day is full of promise and of opportunity. Help me to waste none of it. This day is full of mystery and the unknown. Help me to enjoy it, to face it without fear, anxiety or resentment. This day is full of beauty and adventure. Help me to be fully alive to it all. Remind me throughout this day that it is the journey, not the destination that is to be enjoyed.

Remind me that those who chase security never catch it. I have come to realize that those who believe things will work out, who are willing to be flexible in their plans - that is, those who have faith - have the opportunity to experience serenity and perhaps joy, in this troubled world. Help me with my faith in you.

During this day, may I become a more thoughtful person, a more prayerful person, a more generous and kindly person. Help me to be aware of the feelings of those around me, and provide for them accordingly, through my actions and decisions not to act.

Help me not be turned in toward myself but be sensitive and helpful to others. Let me do nothing today that will harm anyone. Rather let me help, at least a little, to make life more pleasant for those I meet.

Help me to approach my daily tasks with love and a positive attitude, remembering that these tasks are merely a function of existence or survival. They do not define me. Rather, it is my attitude toward these tasks that does.

Make it a day in which I grow more in knowing and accepting your will. Help me accept that "Thy will be done." Thank you for those times when our will's match.

Help me not to worry, not to control, not to take so much responsibility for what happens today. Help me be an observer who does the next right thing rather than one who must force things into my own selected outcome.

When the end of my day comes, may I look back on it without regret. May I not regret anything I have done or failed to do. May I have already apologized for any misstep I may have made, as I know that the apology helps me more than the person who receives it.

Help me to be grateful and to rest, having lived this day as best I can.

Based on Morning Prayer,
Fr. Gerry Chylko, C.Ss.R.

12 Step Reader

Prayer for my loved ones

Help me to understand and empathize with those closest to me. Remind me that they are, as I am, human beings who are facing the trials and tribulations of life each day, as well as fulfilling the role they have in my life.

Bless them and fill their hearts with your grace that they may know the peace and serenity that only knowing you can bring in this world with all its challenges. Help them with their day, their anxieties and fears, their ailments. Care for them and keep them safe.

Help me to give them the unconditional love they need and deserve.

Thank you for putting them in my life.

12 Step Reader

Prayer of gratitude

Thank you for all you have given me,

    For all you have taken away,

        And for all you have left me with.

Thank you for...

Fr. Gerry Chylko, C.Ss.R.

12 Step Reader

I trust that things will work out.
Whatever happens today will happen and
I will make the best of it.

12 Step Reader

Remember

I was once told to make a list of those who I care for so each day I will be reminded to remember them in my prayers. Over time the list will grow and change. Some will come and some will go, others will remain forever.

Who is on your list?

12 Step Reader

Today

Thank you for this day.
Bless all those who have hurt me or helped me,
All I have hurt or helped,
All those I will encounter.
Help me to be a positive factor in their lives –
today.

Bless all those who are trying to be better people,
And those who have yet to try.
Guide my actions and thoughts.
Help me to not hurt anyone emotionally, physically or
spiritually –
today.

Help me to not waste this day with worry, resentment,
anxiety or fear.
Help me to accept that your will, not my will, be done –
today.

12 Step Reader

Action & Outcome

Actions will occur today, reactions will follow and outcomes will result. Lives will be more or less affected and altered in the process. Allow me to consider the result before initiating the action or response.

Help me to differentiate between wanting it my way and doing the right thing. Allow me to think first of others.

Remind me that sometimes my role is to do nothing. To listen compassionately, acknowledge the situation and do nothing. This is often true when listening to women – especially my wife.

Remind me that the only person I can change is me.

12 Step Reader

Serenity

God, grant me the serenity to accept things and people, especially those I love, knowing that I cannot change them. Allow me the courage to change myself and my thinking - help me to go with the flow. Give me the wisdom to recognize that this is required for my serenity and sanity.

Living one day at a time, enjoying one moment at a time, accepting the hardships of life that get in the way of what I want, turning my will over to you, taking this world as it is, and not expecting it to be as I would want it, in order to achieve serenity and peace of mind.

I trust that you will take care of my real needs if I surrender to these realities, that I may be happy, joyous and free from fear in this life.

(The alternative is to be restless, irritable and discontent.)

12 Step Reader

Chapter 2

Meditations

12 Step Reader

He made me to lie down in green pastures

He leads me beside still waters

He restores my soul

23rd Psalm

12 Step Reader

On meditation

Meditation is a quiet time during which thoughts pass through our minds, and we allow them to keep going.

It is a time when we listen to and feel "the quiet."

How does one listen to quiet? By allowing the noise to pass through.

We are meditating when we relax our muscles and allow our body to give in to gravity. When we un-cross our arms and legs. When we close our eyes and breathe deeply. As thoughts come, as they will, we simply don't dwell on them. We release them.

Meditation is a time when we go inside of ourselves and allow what is there to passively come out.

12 Step Reader

On the actions of others

Help me to understand that the actions of others are a result of their lives and are not meant to help or hurt me. Their behavior is about them and their God. It is about their path. I am merely present to experience it with them. I must be diligent in living consistently according to my principles, regardless of my surroundings.

Help me to have an open mind, to consider all the possibilities, to be considerate of the ideas of others, to accept that there are other ways besides my own. I need to allow others to lead or follow, to be themselves. Relieve me of pressures like worrying about the car behind me, and allow me to be guilt free of the needs others impose on themselves.

My rewards come not from others but from inside of me. Through trying to be tolerant and understanding, patient and calm, I will, in time, become happy and content.

12 Step Reader

On truth

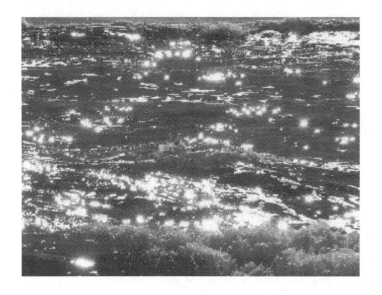

We do not define the truth.
We accept it.

Touchstones

12 Step Reader

I was once told that there are three truths:
Your truth,
My truth and
<u>The</u> truth.

12 Step Reader

Fear

I don't see the fear in other men's hearts because my
own fear is a blinding light.

Fear is the absence of faith.

Help me to feel the freedom that comes from walking
through my fears.

Turn over future fears.

There can be no courage without fear.

12 Step Reader

On worry

I spend so much time re-living yesterday or anticipating tomorrow, that I lose sight of the only time that is really mine - the present moment. You give me today, one moment at a time. That is all I have, all I ever will have.

Give me the faith to know that each moment contains exactly what is to be for me. Help me to look for the good in each encounter of the day. Help me to live it without fear and without guilt.

Give my loved ones and me the hope that comes with trusting you enough to forget past failures and future trials. Help us all find comfort in you for today.

Modified from Morning Prayer, Fr. Gerry Chylko, C.Ss.R.

12 Step Reader

Stop worrying about losing what you have, and start
enjoying it.

Help me to give up worry, remorse, and morbid
reflection for today.
Let me trust in you and enjoy the day.

Help me to accept everyone, and everything, as being as
they should be this day.

12 Step Reader

Mean what you say,
Say what you mean,
But don't say it mean.

12 Step Reader

Reflection on life

I asked God for strength, that I might achieve. I was made weak, that I might learn to let others help me.

I asked God for health, that I might be strong. I was shown illness, that I might understand the true value of life.

I asked God for riches, that I might be secure. I was given less, that I might experience life.

I asked God for power, that I might lead people. It was taken from me, that I might feel the need for God.

I asked for all things, that I might enjoy life. I was given life, that I might enjoy all things*

I got not what I asked for, but everything I hoped for. Despite myself, my prayers were answered. I am, among all people, most richly blessed.

Modified from a Confederate Soldier's Prayer –Author unknown
* From the Book of Solomon

12 Step Reader

First seek to understand – then be kind

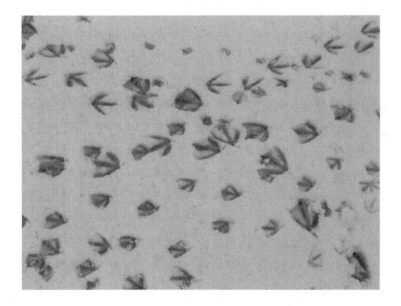

12 Step Reader

Let go and let God

Praying only for knowledge of your will for me,
and the energy, wisdom, and humility
to carry it out.

12 Step Reader

Help me to turn over the anxiety of incomplete tasks,
of outcomes unknown,
of challenges ahead,
of relationships.

12 Step Reader

The question

Do you want to be right?
Or do you want to be happy?

12 Step Reader

On happiness

When you seek happiness for yourself, it will always elude you.

When you seek it for others, you will find it as well.

Wayne Dyer

12 Step Reader

If you cannot be happy with the things you have,

You will not be happy when you get the things you want.

12 Step Reader

Happiness is:
Having someone to love,
Something to do, and
Something to look forward to.

12 Step Reader

On disturbing thoughts

To find peace and serenity, to be happy, I must not harbor disturbing thoughts. Although they come to mind, I must try to let them pass.

If they persist, I must discuss them with those you have put in my life, whom I can trust. I must not keep them inside of me.

I must counter them with constructive and positive thoughts, with thoughts of gratitude, until calmness comes and peace is restored.

The same is true with toxic relationships. I need to avoid those who use and abuse me or those that I love.

12 Step Reader

Humility

Practicing humility allows your higher power to do for
you what you cannot do for yourself.

A lack of humility puts his work on you
and locks him out.

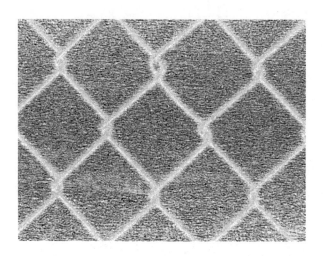

(Humility = Honesty)

12 Step Reader

On rest

Help me to rest,

    To take time to just be me,

        To quiet my mind of thoughts,

            Of obligations, of people,

                Of responsibility.

Relieve me of the fear of failure,

    Allow me to give myself some time,

        To have and savor my blessings,

            And this life of mine.

Beware the temptation of pride,
as the discomfort it brings lasts longer
than the glory

12 Step Reader

On sleep that does not come

I don't understand my inability to sleep, but I try to accept the sleep that does not come.

I ask for help in a brief prayer followed by easy, deep abdominal breathing. I then repeat the Lord's Prayer until sleep comes – and it often does before "...the power and the glory."

At other times I will get up and write my thoughts, or complete a project, go to the living room with a warm beverage and read until my eyes grow weary. I prefer this to lying in bed, tossing and turning.

In all cases I accept this condition, and do what I need to do rather than fight it.

12 Step Reader

A prayer of surrender

I have no idea where I am going. I do not see the road ahead of me. I cannot know for certain where it will end. I have the desire to follow your will - to be a good person, to be humble and charitable, kind and patient, open to others, even if they are different from me. I realize the fact that I think that I am following your will does not mean that I am. However, if I follow what I think is your will for me, I know I am nearer to you, wherever I am.

I believe you will guide and protect me, you will lead me to the right road, and you will care for me in my darkest hour. And while you are doing this, I may know nothing about it, it may be incomprehensible to me, but still I will believe.

I was told that I never have to be alone again and I believe this is true. I believe that you are always there for me, even as I face the darkness. It is through my surrender to you, this belief in a higher power, that I can allay my fears and go forward in this life.

Adapted from Thomas Merton

12 Step Reader

"In surrender there is victory" he said.
He was right.
I just had a hard time accepting it.

12 Step Reader

On restarting my day

Remind me that I can start my day over when things are difficult, or my behavior is unacceptable.

I need to remember that you are there for me to rely on.

I can ask for your help at any time, any place.

It is said that for everything there is a reason.

I need to just look for it, or accept that this is true, and move on.

12 Step Reader

"Life is what happens when you are busy
making other plans."

John Lennon

12 Step Reader

Chapter 3

On God and Spirituality

12 Step Reader

What is awakening within me?
What do you wish me to see?
Where are you leading me?

Be still and know that I am God.

Psalm 46/10

Where are you?
Why are you hiding?

Genesis

Ask not: Is it true?
Ask: What is the truth in it?

Fr. Tom

12 Step Reader

If it turns out that there is no God,
what would you have done differently?

12 Step Reader

On God #1

I was having a difficult time understanding how to relate to God when these thoughts came to me:

It is said that he is infinite and universal and has divine power. It is also said that I am made, as you are, in his image and likeness. Therefore, this power may also be within me, waiting to be called upon, to be deferred to.

Perhaps he lies within me - in the body, mind and spirit; the mind, heart and soul; the id, ego and super ego; the Father, Son and Holy Spirit.

I believe he lies within my subconscious which I cannot comprehend but must seek to communicate with, must believe in.

Not to believe is like denying I have ears.

12 Step Reader

On God #2

If there is a God, a good God, one who loves and cares for us, why do children suffer and die? Why are there wars? Why do clergymen mislead, deceive and hurt us? Why do bad things happen to good people?

Perhaps because we were created with a free will, a blessing and a curse: intelligence and reason, insecurity, envy and jealously, the need to dominate, to survive, to love and lust.

I have the free will to follow these traits, to deal with the world as I choose, as do you. I can try to make it better by trying to make myself better.

We get to adopt our own principles and to live by them.

We need to choose how we will live.

We need to have faith that we can make this a better world, one person at a time.

12 Step Reader

On God #3

"I too struggle with why God allows this (referring to children with cancer). I have come to an understanding within myself. I believe that these are God's children. He put them here not to enjoy this earthly life but to teach us how precious life is. To enable us to be grateful for our lives, our time here and our experiences, all of which these children will have little. They instead, I believe, will soon be where there is no more pain, their mission here on earth having been accomplished."

Benefactor of camp for children with cancer

12 Step Reader

On God #4

...I began to believe that the misery I felt from this endless struggle could be relieved, if I could believe that I was not in charge, that other forces were running the world. Some people said this was God.

One being who is driving all of the events in the world, one who motivates each individual to do the things they do, one who schedules the timing of these actions and who knows, in advance, what is meant to be.

I had trouble with this.

I am not sure there is a God that has a plan. I believe there is one who is benevolent. One who has created man in his own image, each with his own intellect and ability to make good and bad decisions; a God that has given each of us a mind, as well as individual strengths, to deal with this life. One that understands our humanity and forgives us as we try to do the next right thing, even when we don't. One who expects us to forgive our neighbors, and ourselves.

I do not think he plans earthquakes, divorces, deaths and job firings.

12 Step Reader

On God #5

I knew it was a mystery and I honoured it that way.

My grandmother had always referred to the universe as the Great Mystery.

"What does it mean?" I asked her once.

"It means all things."

"I don't understand."

She took my hand and sat me down on a rock at the water's edge. "We need mystery." she said. "Creator in her wisdom knew this. Mystery fills us with awe and wonder. They are the foundations of humility, and humility, grandson, is the foundation of all learning. So we do not seek to unravel this. We honour it by letting it be that way forever."

From *Indian Horse*, a novel by Richard Wagamese
Published by Douglas and McIntyre

12 Step Reader

Is it odd
Or
Is it God?

12 Step Reader

"My sense of God is not as a deity,
But as a profound sense of wonder."

Albert Einstein

12 Step Reader

"Made a decision to turn our lives over to the care of God, as we understand him."

12 & 12

I surrender myself to you to build with me and do with me what you will. I ask that you relieve me of the bondage of self, the stress of being in charge, the egotistical thoughts that fuel my fear and resentments, my vengeance and rage.

Remind me to be humble that I may better do your will. Help me to deal with my difficulties that victory over them may bear witness to those I would help.

Your will, not my will, be done. I am too small a player in this world for it to be otherwise.

12 Step Reader

Another question

TC –   What do you think God's will for you is?

TM –   (after much thought)   I don't know.

TC –   He wants you to be happy, joyous and
              free from fear. He never wants you to be
              alone again. He wants you to experience
              unconditional love, to give it, and
              perhaps, to receive it.

12 Step Reader

Matt Talbot

Matt Talbot (1856 – 1925) was an Irishman who was ruined by drink but recovered through devotion to his God. His devotion went further than most and included self-sacrifice, deprecation, and service as repentance for his drinking life. He inspired the formation of a group dedicated to reuniting its members with God and the Church through retreats which include sharing experiences, meditation, prayer and camaraderie.

Tom C. took me to my first retreat in 1993 at Cor Maria in Sag Harbor. It was through Matt Talbot, and the men I met, that I made my peace with God and the Church after almost 25 years of anger.

There is a small marker and shrine to Matt Talbot at Lourdes Church on Sean McDermott Street in Dublin. To proclaim Matt a saint the Church requires confirmed miracles be witnessed which were brought about through prayer to him. In my opinion he has thousands of miracles, of which I am one.

For more information go to www.MattTalbotRetreats.org

12 Step Reader

Church

Different forms of worship attract different people. There are those who prefer more theatrics, others more tradition, still others who are looking for more theology and some want a closer tie to the good deeds, the helping of one another, we all profess. The binding theme of all Christian churches is that they are structured around Christ as a way of understanding the mysteries of this world.

The Christ story, as told in the four gospels of the New Testament and as predicted in Isaiah of the Old, is the one I grew up with. One I did not question but embraced.

My church added ceremony and a set of rules for conduct to the story, as well as a rating system on bad behavior, all of which I trusted and internalized. This is how I was raised which is why it is "my church."

During those years when I was in the "spiritual debating society," so to speak, I argued with myself over these things that I could not know, could not understand. How can one win an argument when one cannot know? It is a mystery. It is not to be solved but accepted. Accepted on faith, take it or leave it. I left it for a while but had no peace about it.

I have witnessed the power of believing and of accepting over and over again. I found that it is something that I wish to benefit from, so I choose to believe.

I participate in the ceremonies and traditions of my church as I do in my community. I enjoy setting the time aside to worship. I join in the prayers and song, and feel renewed by the physical ingesting of the spirit.

I like helping out with the food pantry, providing for the welfare of others, helping to care for the physical plant. I like the availability of camaraderie, should I choose to avail myself of it. I like recognizing people on the street and in the stores who worship with me. I feel "a part of." I do not see my church as "the" church, but as one of many ways people can connect with a God-based community and each other.

I may not be moved to act on some issues sponsored by the church or to follow all of its dictates. I may be miffed that the church doesn't act on other issues, but no organization can serve all of one's needs and still be a viable organization of more than a few. I accept the limitations of my church and enjoy the rest.

There have been good people, and there have been bad people, associated with church (and worse people who have covered for those bad people). These people, both good and bad, deserve the reputations, the rewards and the punishments commensurate with their actions. They have each passed on to the church that sheltered them their individual reputations, both good and bad. The church is a community of people as much as a way of worship. All communities suffer from their bad apples and church is no different. I have come to realize that men have made mistakes and that church will probably survive those men. Time will tell how well the lessons have been learned.

I was once told to look for the good in organized religion, and take from it what I could. This is how, after much thought and debate, much hurt and hatred, much despair and detestation, I have resolved the unquiet in my heart and can appreciate the good. I have realized that it is by looking for the good rather than fighting that I find peace.

Note: I keep in mind that all churches are interpretations of what man believes God's intention is – and that man is unfailingly fallible. I keep in my heart the God of my understanding.

12 Step Reader

Amazing Grace

Amazing grace, how sweet the sound,
That saved a wretch like me.
I once was lost, but now am found;
Was blind, but now I see.

'Twas grace that taught my heart to fear,
And grace my fears relieved.
How precious did that grace appear,
The hour I first believed.

Through many dangers, toils and snares,
I have already come.
'Tis grace that brought me safe thus far,
And grace will see me home.

12 Step Reader

God's will

It occurred to me, after reading and re-reading, editing and correcting this collection, that I had mentioned and promoted the concept of God's Will and tried to define it as I see it, but that more needed to be said to those who have not been able to grasp the power of the idea.

The skeptic might see this concept as a reason to just not try, to be incapacitated, to wallow in misery, poverty, or the current circumstances - to be passive to the point of self-harm. That is not the intent, in my view.

To me it is more centered on the fact that I am responsible for the effort but not the outcome. I am responsible to try to do what the next right thing is in each aspect of my life, be it personal, family, friends or occupation. What happens next is a fact I have to deal with. I need to accept this outcome as real.

Once having accepted the reality of the situation I may again try to work my way to a different point. I need to reflect on what has occurred, accept that it is due to a combination of my efforts (or lack thereof) and multiple factors from the world at large, God's world, and then determine what I am to do next. More effort, different approach, compromise or adjustment of my goals may be necessary to achieve God's will for me.

Many successful and productive people have accepted "Thy will, not my will, be done." That is: outcomes are driven by many factors, most of which are outside of my ability to control.

I believe God wants me to be happy, joyous and free from fear, to experience serenity. Adopting the above into my thought process and resulting actions gives me the opportunity to realize His will for me.

"Humbly asked him to remove our shortcomings."

12 & 12

I am now willing that you should have all of me, good and bad. I pray that you remove from me every defect of character which stands in the way of my usefulness to you, my family, my fellows and me.

Grant me strength as I go through this life to help me to see the fear under each defect. Help me to perpetually work on these defects and to keep them from entering my thoughts and effecting my actions.

(Our natural state, as alcoholics and addicts, is to be restless, irritable and discontent. The life we have adopted through the 12 Steps and the fellowship of AA gives us the opportunity to be happy, joyous and free from this natural state.)

12 Step Reader

A St. Francis prayer

God, make me a channel of your peace. When I hate, let me try to love. When I injure, let me ask pardon. When I doubt, let me have faith. When I despair, let me hope. When I am in darkness, let me seek light. When I am sad, let me look for joy. When I have resentment, let me understand. When I am jealous, let me feel joy for those I envy.

Help me to give to those I love the unconditional love they deserve. Help me to forgive, as I would want to be forgiven. Grant that I may not so much seek to be consoled, as to console, to be understood, as to understand, to be loved, as to love.

For it is in giving that we receive, in pardoning that we are pardoned, in surrender that we find victory. It is only in dying that we find eternal peace from the struggle of this life so please help me find joy among the realities of each day.

12 Step Reader

Spirituality begins with gratitude

12 Step Reader

Chapter 4

On Work & Making a Living

12 Step Reader

Be content with what you have.
　　　Rejoice in the way things are.

Lao-Tzu

There is more to life than merely increasing its speed.

Gandhi

12 Step Reader

Reflection on material success

As I reflect on riches and poverty, I need to focus not on the relative financial position I am in at work, or in the neighborhood, but rather the position I am in at home, surrounded by the riches that are my family and my friends.

I need to be grateful I am so well off relative to my real needs, both spiritual and material.

I must not let the competitive race, the need to exceed, the size of financial compensation relative to others, the end of a job, the number in line, or the needs and personalities of those around me, ruin the celebration of my good fortune.

12 Step Reader

Tips on the top

When a leader, support those in your charge and give them a chance to grow, even if it is risky for you. This is your responsibility as a leader.

However, realize that there is little sincerity when you are at the top. Do not expect support from those in your work world when you stumble or fall - not even from those you helped.

Conversely, although you may have been loyal to a leader, don't expect loyalty in return when their circumstances or needs change.

Don't be surprised or bitter about it.

Accept this as natural, as the fox who bests the rabbit, or the wolf, the elk, they are only trying to survive.

Just move on. Life is too short for resentment or regret.

(Leadership = Love & Service)

12 Step Reader

The pain of contributing

The need to be right, the desire to control, the suspicion of others motives, all of these create unrest.

I must accept and then contribute.

Contribution without acceptance equals pain. It breeds resentment and resentment poisons the soul.

Humility and gratitude breed serenity.

Serenity is the goal, the big payoff and the true wealth we are all searching for.

Serenity comes from acceptance and gratitude.

I have the choice to accept my circumstances and contribute joyously.

Acceptance is the key.

12 Step Reader

Measure success from within yourself,
based on your own values, rather than those of
others, while being mindful
of their right to measure, as well.

12 Step Reader

On obsession at work

Don't let me obsess on the disorganized, the unfinished or the unfocused.

Help me to accept change and go with it rather than fret over that which was not completed. Help me to take each day as an individual day, one day at a time, one step at a time, one person at a time.

Help me not put too much value on the plans of men in the face of your will for us.

I cannot see into the hearts of other men nor can I know their minds. If coworkers are not comfortable with the sincerity and intention of my efforts, help me to accept this or to find a place to apply my gifts in a positive way - if it be your will.

Remind me that there is no end to this game called work. Help me to play it as best I can, without sacrificing my principles, my family or myself.

12 Step Reader

On dealing with the work world

I pray for the knowledge that my job is the work you have for me to do. Help me do it well.

I pray for the courage, insight and conviction to change myself, to be flexible in my work. Give me the strength to remain willing to put in the effort, to walk through my fears and resentments.

I pray for an understanding of my responsibilities, and the ability to be satisfied while meeting my obligations.

I pray that I may enjoy my daily work and benefit those I encounter.

I pray that I understand and accept when other people do not understand or support my opinions and decisions. Help me to appreciate and respect their perspective.

Help me to understand when my job comes to an end and allow me to leave with dignity.

I pray for patience, and trust that all will be well.

12 Step Reader

We fought everyday realities
as if they were personal enemies.

Touchstones

12 Step Reader

I have a mission

You created me to do some definite service. You have committed some work to me which you have not committed to another. I have a mission.

I am a link in a chain, a bond of connection between persons. You have given me this opportunity for a reason, therefore I will trust you, whatever, wherever I am.

When I am mission-less

Though my work be taken away,
Though I feel desolate,
Though my spirits sink,
Though my future be hidden from me,
I will trust you.

If I am confused and uncertain I trust that, in time, you will clarify things for me.

I need to make the best of what I am served.

Modified from Cardinal Newman

12 Step Reader

On faith

I often think of Wayne.

He left a long term position (as a printer), and took
another position to improve his lot.

He was fired from his new position and was out of work.

He eventually got another job, under worse conditions,
and was sure it all happened for a reason.

I have always admired his faith.

12 Step Reader

Thank you for my work

Thank you for the life you have given me,

For my family and friends,

My home and community,

And my ability to make a living.

Thank you for my work,

For the challenges,

And experiences you have provided.

Thank you for all these things.

12 Step Reader

On achieving goals

Knowing how to turn things over to you

Knowing that effort and intent, not outcome, are what belong to me

Knowing that others will usually do what they perceive to be best for themselves

Knowing that the material is not a significant reward when one must sacrifice the spirit, the heart, the self, and the family

Knowing that I tend to obsess on my vision of what could or should be, and it blinds me to other things I should see and understand

Knowing that some will resent me for the good I do as well as the mistakes I make

Knowing that some will withhold their support in order to maintain their edge

Knowing these things and still wanting to be a worker among workers, if it be your will

12 Step Reader

Self-centered

Self-centeredness makes us
take everything personally. It makes us hypersensitive
to our surroundings, other people and what they think,
how they behave, how they react. Yet most of the time
these things have very little to do with us. The work
world with its bosses, plans, employees, customers, and
suppliers all goes on as it will for its own reasons.
Thinking we can change all of these
people and things to our way
of thinking is not healthy.
All we can do is try to go
with the flow, do the
next right thing
and possibly
help meet
the needs
of those
who rely
on
us.

12 Step Reader

Our self-importance requires that
we spend most of our lives
offended by someone.

Touchstones

12 Step Reader

Chapter 5

A Way of Life

12 Step Reader

Do I have the patience to wait until the mud settles and the water is clear?

Can I remain unmoving until the right action arises by itself?

Tao Te Ching

It is better to want what you have than to have what you want.

Dalai Lama

Acceptance

Acceptance is the answer to all of my problems.

When I am disturbed it is because I find some person, place, situation or thing – some fact of my life – unacceptable to me.

I can find no serenity until I accept that person, place, situation or thing as being exactly the way it is supposed to be – at this moment in time.

It is from this acceptance that I will grow, that my life will take form, that my character will be molded.

My actions will dictate the next step in my life.

I need only to deal with these things as they are, to seek ways to address them constructively, to use them to learn more about myself.

I need to go forward without the urge to control, without resentment, without anxiety, without fear.

Adapted from the BB, 3rd edition, pg. 449

12 Step Reader

A way of living – a letter to my sons

After over 60 years on this earth, I have come to understand a few basic principles that are the key to my happiness and success. It is nothing like what I thought it would be, but it is what has made all the difference in my life.

I want to share these principles with you and, if the time is right, perhaps they can affect your life in as positive a way as they have mine.

After some very difficult years of endless fighting and straining, trying to figure out what one is supposed to do to succeed in this world, I came to understand and accept that I did not have the power I thought I had. My personal and business life was not a manageable thing to be controlled to suit my fancy. Things just didn't seem to go my way, although I tried endlessly to see that they did. I had to surrender to the fact that I cannot control my world. It was a devastating realization.

I began to believe that the misery I felt from this endless struggle could be relieved if I could grasp that I was not in charge, that other forces were running the world. Some people said this was God. One being who is driving all the events in the world, one that motivates

151

each individual to do the things they do, and one who schedules the timing of all actions. One who knows in advance what will happen.

I had trouble with this.

I am not sure there is a God that has a plan. I believe there is one who is benevolent and who has created man in his own image, each with his own intellect and ability to make good and bad decisions; a God that has given each of us a mind as well as individual talents to deal with this life. One that understands our humanness and forgives us as we try to do the next right thing, even when we don't, and one who expects us to forgive our neighbors as well as ourselves. However, I do not think he plans earthquakes, divorces, deaths and job firings.

I had a wonderful faith and love for God when I was a child, and even as a young adult. I thought he abandoned me in 1969. It took me a long time to trust in him again. I worked hard on my faith, and it has returned to me, not the pure faith of a child, but an adult version.

Once I began to understand that I was but a small player in this universe, that I was not meant to control it, and that worry about the whys and wherefores did me no good, there was nothing left to do but the next right thing, and to try to smell the roses each day.

Sounds naïve but it works.

I had to be honest with myself about who I really am and what I have done to contribute to the pain in my life. I came to realize that I was not always right. I had some character flaws that repeatedly beat me down; flaws that made it difficult for me to get along in this world, and difficult to experience peace and happiness.

I found someone to share these thoughts with, someone who I trusted and to whom I could tell anything. Someone who would be a good listener, not a judge. Someone who would point out the defects in my character in an honest and loving way so that I could see them, and begin to work on them. This enabled me to try to give them up, these defects, this flawed thinking, which had dominated my life. It allowed me to begin to change.

I realized that my upbringing, my genetics and my personality all contributed to these defects, as well as to all of my positive attributes. I knew I needed help to work on myself. I asked God to help me not be whoever I was when my character defects came out. I continued to talk to trusted friends about it.

In addition I have tried to incorporate the following tenets into my life:

I realized that anger and hate have no place in my life. There is no such thing as justified anger – all anger does is hurt me. It is self-inflicted pain. Grudges do no one any good. It was amazing to me when I realized that anyone I was mad at owned my mind and energy. Why would I give all this to someone I did not care for? It took me a long time to realize how true this was. It is much better to forgive and pray for the well-being of those who hurt me, for then I heal and feel better. Today I pray for my enemies.

I now begin and end each day with a prayer of gratitude. I thank God for the sunrise, for the family I have, for my home, my pet and my friends. I thank him for being so well off in this world where there is so much horror, so many with so little, so many living under terrible conditions, so many who have tortured minds, so many who cannot face the day with any joy.

I thought about people and organizations who may have been hurt when my character defects took over. I decided to forgive those that had hurt me and, when possible, made amends to those I hurt.

On most days, when I become agitated, I take time to reflect before I respond. I call to mind the gratitude I have. I think about the next right thing to do.

When I act poorly, I try to quickly recover, to say I am sorry, and to right the situation.

I try to remember what is really important in this life – it is not work, or money, or anything other than love. Love is something I have to give. I cannot sit around and hope to receive it.

I find time for myself. I treat myself to some peace and quiet. I let thoughts come and go. I meditate or sit quietly at least once each day. It centers me. It prepares me for what life is going to do next.

I try to help others. I am not always successful but I try. I try to be there for my wife, my children and their families.

I try to be aware of my internal limits. Sometimes I need to recharge my batteries. I need to get out of bad relationships, be they personal or on the job, for these drain me. They take the love I have to give and squander it.

I need to remind myself that I can be self-destructive and need to guard against hurting myself.

I hope you can find your way to whatever gives you the serenity, peace and love you need and deserve. Just know that it is not to be found in material things or in your position in society. It can be achieved under most any circumstances for you carry it with you at all times.

You just need to allow it to come out. You just need to accept it.

Dad

Make it your daily goal
To do good deeds and not get caught

12 Step Reader

On dealing with people

People are hard to love. They are often unreasonable, illogical and self-centered.
>Love them anyway.

If you do well, people will accuse you of selfish ulterior motives. Some will take advantage of you, and some won't understand.
>Do well anyway.

If you are successful, you will win false friends and true enemies.
>Succeed anyway.

The good work you do today will be forgotten tomorrow.
>Do it anyway.

Honesty makes you vulnerable.
>Be honest anyway.

Your most creative ideas can be shot down by people who lack your vision.
>Be creative anyway.

What you spend years building may be destroyed overnight.

>Build anyway, for you love to build.

People really need help, but may attack those who help them.

>Offer to help them anyway.

Give the job the best you've got and you may get kicked in the teeth.

>Give it your best anyway.

People will label you, and try to keep you in your place.

>Seek out your own labels.

The bottom line when dealing with people is to follow the golden rule…

>And wear a helmet.

Modified from Karl A. Menninger's 80th birthday letter

Open minded

"Being open minded is like this" she said: "When you are absolutely certain that you are 100% right you stop and consider that maybe, just maybe, the other person may be right as well."

12 Step Reader

Suggestions for living

Spend time with nature, not controlling it or trying to conquer it, but understanding and appreciating that you are part of it, and that it goes on as it will.

Be generous. Give every day. Give emotionally, materially and spiritually. Be caring, affectionate, and empathetic toward others. Be generous without seeking reward. Give of your time and your money. Give for the good of others, without ulterior motives. Give to those in need either directly or through organizations. Donate to causes you believe in. Donate often and with generosity.

Even if you are limited in income, consider how much money you waste on junk each day, and how much better that money would have been used if channeled to a cause you care about. As bad off as you may think you are, there are others much worse off. Give to remind yourself of this. Find ways to give of yourself, of your time.

Show appreciation and graciously accept that which is given to you, as well. Learn to simply say "thank you."

Don't fight everything. Accept the present moment as it is and move on. Let it go. Fighting everything wastes energy and energy is your life.

The ego expends the most energy, and does the least good. Seeking power or control over others, or seeking the approval of others, is a function of ego and wastes energy.

Allow others the freedom to be as they are. Don't judge. If they are not good for you, move on rather than trying to change or control them. Don't gossip about them. Just move on.

Those who seek security (i.e. money) chase it for their lifetime. There is never enough. I recall the story of a financial trader who made it from nowhere to the list of the 25 richest people in the USA. He was said to be upset that he was on the bottom of the list. Enjoy the challenge and excitement of your current situation. Remember life is a journey, and you don't want to arrive at the station too soon.

To find your purpose in life (not OF life which is beyond our comprehension) focus on what you have to give. Develop your talents and apply them to serve humanity.

Reflect on "Ask not what your country can do for you but rather what you can do for your country" (JFK) and insert whatever word is applicable in place of "country" such as "family," "parents," "friend," "spouse," "job," "community," "children," etc.

Remember, we all have different gifts. Realize that your talents may or may not be related to your making a living. They may instead be in your ability to be a good parent, a good friend, a good neighbor. Don't expect your gifts to always compliment the market place or the goals of others.

Inspired by The Seven Spiritual Laws –
Deepak Chopra

12 Step Reader

Those who forget the past are condemned to
repeat it – or worse

G. Santayana

Brotherhood

Regardless of our prayers, I am not sure God will fix the horrors of our world. Our free will seems to have condemned us to live with the short comings of ourselves and others. All we can do is to try to live each day without the fear-driven hate that fouls our world - and too many of us.

We seem to have a natural instinct to hate those who are not like us; those who look different, live different, speak different, think different. We make hurtful jokes and pass them on. We laugh when others tell them.

We always seem to need someone, or some group, to blame – especially for those things we cannot understand or control. Hate is the result, blind, unconditional hate of individuals we don't even know - never met.

Those of us who have had the blessing of the rooms of AA know how much alike we all are. We need to let this knowledge carry through to the other aspects of our lives and all of our other relationships.

If we could do that the brotherhood of man just might become a reality – one person at a time.

12 Step Reader

On character

You refuse to take the extra change the cashier gives you by mistake – Or you keep it rationalizing that the store can afford it and you need it more than they do.

You pick up some litter because you appreciate the natural beauty of an area and don't want it marred by trash – Or you throw trash out the window because you want a clean car for yourself.

You take the time to really listen to a child's question and try to give them a reasonable and responsible answer – Or you turn everything into a joke to cover your own ignorance or impatience.

You allow the car trying to get on the highway to pull in – Or you pass standing traffic on the shoulder because it is important that you get to where you are going, regardless of others.

You look around your home and thank God for all you have been given – Or you are constantly focused on the house up the street, wanting what they have.

What is your character?

When all else fails –

Do unto others, as you would have others
do unto you.

12 Step Reader

Reading List and Sources

When I read books, especially the self-help or spiritual type, I try to look for insights, and to expand my world view. I don't look for an instruction manual. I don't expect it to have all the answers. I don't expect to agree with it all. But if I get one thought out of each book, one clarification of how I feel, it was well worth the time and effort. There is no single magic answer for everyone in any of the books listed (except for the last two), but I found them all worth re-reading.

In The Spirit of Our Program – Fr. Gerry Chylko, C.Ss.R., www.MattTalbotRetreats.org

Touchstones –A daily reader for men - Hazelden Press

Breathing Under Water – Richard Rohr – Franciscan Media

First You Have to Row a Little Boat – Richard Bode – Warner Books

How Good Do We Have to Be? – Harold S. Kushner – Little Brown

Conversations with God - Book 1 - Neale Donald Walsch – Putnam

The Sermon on the Mount – Emmet Fox – Harper Collins

Don't Sweat the Small Stuff – Richard Carlson – Hyperion

Manifest Your Destiny – Wayne Dyer – Harper Collins

The Seven Spiritual Laws of Success – Deepak Chopra – New World Library

Alcoholics Anonymous – (aka BB – the Big Book)

Twelve Steps and Twelve Traditions – Alcoholics Anonymous

This book is published as a collection of thoughts, prayers and meditations and distributed for the benefit of all who are open to a spiritual life and in the hope that more will discover what I have been blessed with.

Available on Amazon.com
In print and digital

Comments and inquiries are welcome at
Tomsbooks@optonline.net

(Note: In the "first printing" of this book, I had placed my initials after what I considered original work. Over time I have come to realize that even the most original pieces were influenced by all my other reading and most have sources, although they are unknown to me. My apologies to any author I may have used as the basis for those pieces.)

COMPASSION – *Think about it*

12 Step Reader

Your thoughts:

Made in the USA
San Bernardino, CA
26 June 2018